TWENTY FOUR PRELUDES AND FUGUES ON DMITRI SHOSTAKOVICH

Joanna Boulter

TWENTY FOUR PRELUDES AND FUGUES ON DMITRI SHOSTAKOVICH

2006

Published by Arc Publications
Nanholme Mill, Shaw Wood Road
Todmorden OL14 6DA, UK
www.arcpublications.co.uk

Copyright © Joanna Boulter 2006
Design by Tony Ward
Printed by Biddles Ltd
King's Lynn, Norfolk, UK

ISBN-13: 978 1904614 34 0
ISBN-10: 1 904614 34 5

ACKNOWLEDGEMENTS:
The poem 'Fugue "Don't take those mittens off..."' appeared in a souvenir programme for a Shostakovich concert at the City of London Festival on 22 July 2005, and was subsequently broadcast when this concert was heard on BBC Radio 3, on 3 August 2005.

Cover photograph © Alan Turnbull,
'Mikhailovsky Gardens, St. Petersburg'

All rights reserved. No part of this book may be reproduced or duplicated in any form without prior permission from the publishers.

The Publishers acknowledge financial assistance from ACE Yorkshire

Editor for the UK and Ireland: Jo Shapcott

Contents

Author's Preface / 7
Praeludium / 11
Prelude 'Frost flowers...' / 12
Fugue 'Don't take those mittens off ...' / 13
Prelude 'Light burned the sky...' / 14
Fugue 'Our job is to rejoice...' / 15
Prelude 'Endemic...' / 16
Canon: *Ascendente Modulatione* / 17
Prelude 'snatch of music...' / 18
Fugue 'Sometimes I can be calm...' / 19
Prelude on a Chorale / 20
Double Fugue / 21
Prelude *quasi madrigale* / 24
Fughetta / 25
Prelude 'The necessary illusion...' / 26
Fugue of the Cinema Pianist / 27
Motherlove / 28
Prelude im Volkston / 30
Fugue 'A winter's tale...' / 31
Kolybel'naya / 33
Prelude 'Remember being young?...' / 34
Fuga Enharmonica / 35
Contradanza / 36
Prelude 'So, who do you suppose...' / 37
Fugue on DSCH / 39
Prelude of the Apparatchiks for Babi Yar / 40
Fugue 'Most of my symphonies...' / 41
Interlude / 42
Prelude 'Well, we're all in the same boat...' / 44

Fugue 'To compose only what you want to compose...' / 45
Underground / 46
Tunguska Incident / 47
Prelude on the Zdanov Decree / 48
Fugue 'You are a vicious formalist...' / 49
Tenth Symphony / 50
Recitative / 51
Arioso / 52
Lament / 53
A Scapegoat / 54
Prelude after Akhmatova / 55
Fugue 'Not demons but despairs...' / 56
Prelude 'The Little Spring...' / 57
Mirror Fugue / 58
Two-part Invention / 60
Fugue of the Former Students of Shostakovich... / 62
Stalin as Heldentenor / 64
The Death of Stalin / 65
The Pupil Remembers / 67
Soliloquy / 69
Chaconne / 71
Coda / 73

Biographical note / 75

Author's Preface

In 1994 I read a review by Peter Conrad, in *The Observer*, of Elizabeth Wilson's *Shostakovich: A Life Remembered*. As its title suggests, this is a compendium of personal reminiscences by relatives, friends and acquaintances of the composer. The glimpses of Shostakovich's life which the review quoted caught my imagination as a possible subject for poetry, and I began what quickly became a lengthy project. Conrad's reference to Shostakovich's *24 Preludes & Fugues op. 87* for piano gave me my format. I decided to write a set of twenty four preludes and fugues myself, in words – the preludes in free or invented forms, in the third person, and the fugues in any strict poetic form, in the first person, as the voice of Shostakovich himself. In practice, this plan relaxed somewhat as the work progressed.

I have been asked how closely these poems echo Shostakovich's *Preludes and Fugues*. The answer is, only in the most general terms. It proved too difficult to make each pair of poems shadow the mood and, still more, the musical content of a corresponding pair of piano pieces, and in the end I didn't try. Since music, after all, functions as a representation rather than a precise description, to align the poetry strictly with the music would have left me without much narrative possibility. I needed to be be able to refer to other works of his, and other periods of the composer's life.

I'm indebted to the following books, and to many other references in print, on the internet, and on radio, for information and insight. All of these constantly reminded me that the historic events of the twentieth century in the U.S.S.R. involved not just a huge nation but real individual human beings.

Ardov, Revd. Michael, translated by Rosanna Kelly and Michael
    Meylac, *Memories of Shostakovich: Interviews with the composer's children* (Short Books, 2004);
Fay, Laurel E., *Shostakovich: A Life* (Oxford University Press
    Inc., 2000);

Glikman, Isaak, translated by Anthony Phillips, *Story of a Friendship: the Letters of Dmitry Shostakovich to Isaak Glikman* (Faber & Faber, 2001);
Volkov, Solomon, translated by Antonina W. Bouis *Testimony: The Memoirs of Dimitri Shostakovich* (Faber & Faber, 1987);
Wilson, Elizabeth, *Shostakovich: A Life Remembered* (Faber & Faber, 1994).

*

I would like to thank Northern Arts for a Tyrone Guthrie residency, New Writing North for a Northern Promise award, and The Hawthornden Trust for a Fellowship. All of these gave me much-appreciated support, both financial and practical.

In particular, I wish to thank David Morley for his invaluable help and advice.

The friendship and encouragement of S. J. Litherland, Annie Wright, and especially my husband Roger Collett have been and continue to be indispensable.

TWENTY FOUR PRELUDES AND FUGUES ON DMITRI SHOSTAKOVICH

PRÆLUDIUM

The dark is always worst. Somewhere,
for someone, night's rhythms will solidify
into the knock on the door.
And someone starts up scattering the patience cards,
leans a moment against the wall before walking
with stiff knees and shaking breath towards the sound.
This country lives
in the heartbeat before Beethoven's fate motif,
on a perpetual inbreath hurting the diaphragm.
There are so many ways of being wrong.

Prelude
for a hard winter

Frost flowers all day long on the window-panes.
She ekes fuel till the children come,
still in her coat and shawl, chopping shrunk potatoes,
a single saved onion. Cold sharpens the knife.
When she can get more tea she'll invite friends –
talk warms the heart, as breath and bodies do
the room. But not tonight. She rakes the stove,
coaxes embers with cloud-breath. A frail flame
stabs at the air. The ice-flowers bruise a little.
Snow swirls outside. She stirs the meagre soup,
cuts a ration of coarse bread, not enough
for children's appetites. And here they come,
scurrying bright-eyed through winter, laughing,
one glove shared turnabout between four hands.

Fugue

Don't take those mittens off until you're called
to play your bit. Blow on your fingers, tuck
them in your armpits, beat this vicious cold
how best you can. Music's what matters. Look,

the carvings on the wall are rimmed with rime.
The keyboard's icy too. It hurts to play.
So what? Think of the music as a flame
to warm your spirit at. That's what I do.

There's counterpoint and cabbage soup, there's Bach
and badinage; and if that's not enough
you needn't stay. Okay, the winter's harsh.
And so am I. Get on and do your stuff.

The profs may make allowances. I don't.
And you delude yourself, for music can't.

Prelude
after Hiroshima

Light burned the sky, a conflagration
of warrior angels: the earth shook.
Shaken and blinded by this resolution
our job is to rejoice.

Each burning child was seared onto the pavement,
each frantic parent fled in vain.
Ablaze, transformed by such a resolution
our job is to rejoice.

Cities were sudden rubble. Bones crumbled
to brittle foundations at the quiet voice
commanding war to such a resolution.
Our job is to rejoice.

These deaths are branded on our hearts for ever,
blood-bonded by the hurt we shared.
Though all are blinded by that resolution
our job is to rejoice.

Fugue

Our job is to rejoice. Simple C major?
That resolution cost me so much blood.
My music's comfort for that fiery child
would seem to him no more than a betrayer.
And yet: Our job is to rejoice. Each player
phrases his personal anguish to enfold
the pain of others, till he bleeds aloud
through every note. And still: simple C major.

Better to starve in Leningrad than burn?
I wouldn't know. The world is full of grief.
All I can do is hear the weeping voice;
wrestle the discords into unison,
transpose Hiroshima to flute's cool breath
singing with me: Our job is to rejoice.

Prelude

Endemic, this malaria of suspicion.
As if the land's one vast mephitic swamp,
rumours buzzing like mosquitoes. Someone
scratches an itch, and before you can say *Lubianka*
another poor devil's in quarantine.
It's a contagion. You can't tell who's clean.
Often they show no symptoms till they fall,
are lugged off, screaming, fainting, in the plague cart.
And the relatives, too – for every mother
queueing those lifetimes at the iron doors
a dozen cousins withdraw themselves from taint,
lay information for a talisman.
The witchfinders search for infection, stalk the streets,
all bone masks and blank eyes in the night.
And the lost behind those high walls dwindle away,
all bone masks, blank eyes, forgotten names.

Canon: *Ascendente Modulatione*

Comrade Zanchevsky's summons. Him! Arrested,
just as I'd feared. It had to come some day.
Leaving the house was part of being tested,
my hands all sweating and my mouth all dry.

Just as I'd feared, it had to come some day.
We only talked of music, I protested,
my hands all sweating and my mouth all dry.
Stalin was never mentioned, I insisted,

we only talked of music. I protested.
My work, my wife, my child. What dared I say?
Stalin was never mentioned, I insisted.
Me, a grown man, determined not to cry.

My work, my wife, my child – what could I say?
Leaving the house was part of being tested,
me, a grown man, and frantic not to cry.
– Comrade Zanchevsky's summons? *Him*, arrested?

Prelude
Staccato leggierissimo

snatch of music   turn the dial
        (*hissing*)   becoming
                            laughter
a voice (*crackle*) speaks
    gabbles gibberishBLAREjazzband *quick*
                    the volume
          turn
      more soundwaves roar
            the pointer (*hisses*) glides   dangerously
home

English Received Pronunciation   frog in throat

                            unsafe
    to tune ears to   this
                    quick
        back
    through
  (*crackling*)   static
    to the home
station

              no-one must know

Fugue

Sometimes I can be calm inside my shell,
cool down each nerve, draw back my horns again
within myself. Safer to be a snail.

I know it's an imaginary wall
and frail as well; but better that than none.
Sometimes I can be calm inside my shell.

There's a full orchestra, untouchable,
filling my head, and all for me to tune
within myself. Safer to be a snail.

And for a while it suits me very well
to keep my naked thinking solely mine.
Sometimes I can be calm inside my shell.

They can't get at me there. How can they tell
what music's going on inside my brain,
within myself? Safer to be a snail,

cool down each nerve, draw back my horns again;
ignore the pain of fear, the fear of pain
within myself. Safer to be a snail.
Sometimes I can be calm inside my shell.

Prelude on a Chorale
The Revolution of 1917

>   *Could architecture, could the alphabet,*
>   *art's formal civilities, comprehend*
>   *the scale of it, mass-murder's tonic solfa,*
>   *a bloody gamut in perpetual round?*

Not honourable listings. Not glorious fallen.
Graffiti of threat on theatre walls
>   *Could architecture, could the alphabet,*
meticulously listed. These are called Enemies
of the People. Such temporary archives,
>   *art's formal civilities, comprehend*
the names bleeding from pillar to pillar.
Live blood runs cold. A nightmare
>   *the scale of it, mass-murder's tonic solfa,*
pitched too high. Wake sweating. So many names.
One might be yours. When did the struggle become
>   *a bloody gamut in perpetual round?*
a vicious score? Begun in hope
why should it ever stop?

Double Fugue

EXPOSITION I

Picture the scene. A workers' demonstration
there in the dusk, half-starved, ill-clad and cold,
that February. Police in ranks untold
stood rigid till you could have plucked the tension,
until the crack of nerves. Then sabres slashing
swooped, hacked at the helpless. Black blood pooled:
a boy fell dying, nothing but a child –
I watched him, tearful in my safe compassion.

He was my age. It's not the sort of thing
I could forget. If only I believed
the martyrdom, the undue reckoning
won't be forgotten. He was just my age,
and I must think more than his mother grieved
when he was cut to ground, at that outrage.

EXPOSITION II

An icon, printed on my haunted eye,
– though I may not have seen it, there's some doubt,
it might have been something I'd read about –
the uniforms, the weapons to defy
innocent flesh. Surely I heard the cry:
not anger, but despair. In all that rout
you'd think we were too young to be late out;
and he was certainly too young to die.

Although I maybe wasn't there in fact
the vivid horror of that bloody street
lives on as though I'd seen it in the act,
so that I keep on hearing like a dream
above the ostinato booted feet
the descant of his piccolo scream.

STRETTO

Picture this scene. A workers' demonstration
    An icon, printed on my haunted eye,
there in the dusk, half-starved, ill-clad and cold,
    – though I may not have seen it, there's some doubt,
that February. Police in ranks untold
    it might have been something I'd read about –

stood rigid till you could have plucked the tension,
> *the uniforms, the weapons to defy*
until the crack of nerves. Then sabres slashing
> *innocent flesh. Surely I heard the cry:*
swooped, hacked at the helpless. Black blood pooled;
> *not anger, but despair. In all that rout*
a boy fell dying, nothing but a child –
> *you'd think we were too young to be late out;*
I watched him, tearful in my safe compassion
> *and he was certainly too young to die.*

He was my age. It's not the sort of thing
> *Although I maybe wasn't there in fact*
I could forget. If only I believed
> *the vivid horror of that bloody street*
the martyrdom, the undue reckoning
> *lives on as though I'd seen it in the act,*
won't be forgotten. He was just my age –
> *so that I keep on hearing like a dream*
and I must think more than his mother grieved
> *above the ostinato booted feet*
when he was cut to ground, at that outrage
> *the descant of his piccolo scream.*

Prelude *quasi madrigale*
Allegretto semplice

As new as every wave
as ancient as the sea

as fresh as tender leaves
as stalwart as a tree

as hopeful as each day
lighting skies above

this is the old, old way
when youth and maiden love.

Fughetta

A trio for first love. The best of me
so far, although this won't be so for long.
Here all is holiday, here we are free.
But youthful rhapsody
must be transposed to a more formal key.
She burst me into song,
and this our firstborn has to grow. Though we
won't change our hearts, my music can't stay young.

Prelude

The necessary illusion. When times are hard
and hungry, and the good things
(though of course your faith in them wouldn't
falter) seem to take their time arriving, it's
the silver screen that makes the difference.
Reality and *the vision*. Just for a bit
they're the same thing; and there in the warm dark
while the beam flickers and the hero is martyred
and the radiant workers toil and march
arm in arm towards the bright dream
all the ideals glow and flow together
till the whole cinema's filled with brotherhood.

Fugue of the Cinema Pianist

Da capo drudgery, night after night.
And there's so much to learn, so little time
for my own music; but we have to eat.

I got some friends in, tried my trio out.
There were complaints. Just someone who can strum
da capo drudgery, night after night.

And add to that, the manager's a cheat
and wouldn't pay. I tell you, I could scream
for my own music; but we have to eat,

and though I'm wasting vital time, I've got
to do it. They rely on me at home.
Da capo drudgery, night after night,

night after night. I'm sitting here, dead beat,
without a pause to summon up a theme
for my own music. But we have to eat,

and music paper costs, and there are debts;
and since my father died I've much less time
for my own music. But we have to eat.
So, back to drudgery, night after night.

Motherlove

I started all three of them on the piano
at the age of nine. I don't believe in forcing
a child too young. And they were all musical, of course,
but the boy was something special; it was evident
at once that he was seriously gifted.
Playing four-handed duets with me
after two days! perfect pitch! And notation!
you'd think that, rather than learning it,
he was remembering something from an earlier life.
Soon he was composing little tunes.

That girl was no good for him, though.
Don't get me wrong, I didn't care if he screwed her;
but that didn't give her the right to his time.
Nights, maybe; but remember he's a genius,
and a genius needs his sleep. That's
what I told her. And he said
Tanya is good for me, she soothes me,
I can work when she's there. She, of course,
believed him. But I wasn't fooled.
Sitting up against him at the table, hair
all over the music, thigh pressed against his –
oh, the trollop didn't fool me for a second!
But she'd got him by the balls all right.
In the end, though,
he had the sense not to marry her. Not
that the one he did pick was any more biddable,
and she fancied herself as a pianist!
think of it, a piano-playing physicist!

But though she got upset at his high spirits
(and she should have expected *that,* with a genius)
her parents wouldn't let her divorce him,
clung on like death itself
knowing he was marked for fame.
They were always a pushy lot, that family.

Prelude im Volkston

The rivers slow to silence under ice.
Who can tell how they preserve their life?

An evil magician holds the land in thrall
and winter snarls beside him like a wolf.

When will the spell be broken? Not until
a singer comes with his enchanted harp

to tune the icicles and voice the wind
so silver music melts the frozen heart.

The river slowed to silent under ice.
A golden sturgeon sings out of its deeps.

Fugue

A winter's tale. Beleaguered Leningrad
circled by hate and belted in with hunger
under the enemy's cold watchful eye,
across the frozen Neva. Icicles
are stronger weapons than the guns, but hope
battles privation in those dogged hearts.

So how shall I compose, seeing my heart's
as frozen as this ink? All Leningrad
looks towards me, it seems, to give them hope,
a finished symphony for spirits' hunger
composed with pain, sharp as an icicle.
Though I'm now safe, these people fill my eyes.

Some news gets out. They're clear in my mind's eye:
little to burn for fires to cheer their hearts,
but where they can they're melting icicles
for drinking-water now in Leningrad,
trapping rats and mice to ease their hunger,
enduring, trusting to the spring for hope

though summer's scarcely better. A faint hope
must have been kindled as the sun's bright eye
first thawed the snowy city. But their hunger
eats cardboard, paper, substance without heart;
and there are no cats left in Leningrad.
For famine pierces like an icicle

and cuts them to the quick, an icicle
that's called despair. It's slowly freezing hope.
The Philharmonic's gone from Leningrad,
leaving these few musicians, sunken-eyed,
infirm of fingers though more stout of heart,
an orchestra of players faint with hunger.

For there are other needs and other hungers
that drive us all. Despite the icicles
the music flows, alive, from heart to hearts,
my gift to bring a suffering people hope.
The hall is full. There isn't a dry eye
now for this symphony, my *Leningrad*,

that feeds their hunger with the meat of hope,
melting the icicle inside the eye,
to give them back their hearts in Leningrad.

Kolybel'naya

CRADLE SONG

No room
in that crowded train
to rock a child
spi, malutka

It's the bond
of family
that rocks a child
spi, malutka

How can I shield them
protect them
rock my children?
spi, malutka

I can't protect myself.
Let me survive
until they're old enough
spi, spi, malutka

spi, malutka – sleep, little one

Prelude

Remember being young? how works of art
burst on you like the rising of the sun,
lighting the whole horizon? Or as if
the first fresh flower of spring revealed itself
to you alone? Now growing minds light up
at Shostakovich and Akhmatova,
those vivid blossoms lovely in themselves,
heralds of more to come.

But now we're told such plants are dangerous
with twisted growth; that they can only yield
poisonous flowers, rank honey, corrupt fruit.
We teach our children caution, watch them learn
to check response and curb their puzzled hearts.
And it's as if winter should spring from spring,
shrivelling back into the blackened branch
a resurrection's green.

Fuga Enharmonica

I am a falling star, forced from its orbit.
I had my place in the cosmology,
but Lucifer-like I'm declining from it.
And turbulent influences prophesy
disjointed seasons. To reclassify
one steady star an inauspicious comet
changes the constellation, the whole sky
and all direction-finding sighted on it.

I haven't moved an inch. My music's still
just what it was. Yet something's out of tune,
somehow the key has changed, to undermine
my harmony and wrench it from its scale;
and all I do seems only to decline
to interrupted cadence, dying fall.

Contradanza

These are the figures of the dance. Stalin advances
towards me. I retreat. Then he draws back.

I tiptoe forwards. This pattern we're making
satisfies him. It keeps me on the hop.

What's not allowed
is to sit the whole bloody masquerade out.

No wallflowers here! he cries: *Get up! get up!*
He'll dance with me himself.

Prelude

So, who do you suppose paid for your talent?
Not you, boy; not your parents.

Who trained you? fed you with extra rations?
You'd have died as a student

when the tuberculosis swelled your neck,
without that post-operative stay

in the expensive State Sanatorium,
the convalescence by the Black Sea –

from which came . . . ? only
"a trio for first love"!

Better watch your step, boy!
We could still cut your throat.

Who spirited you out of Leningrad
in spite of the insult of that opera?

Don't you think we have the right
to expect some gratitude,

some music to express the soul of your people
instead of this selfish "self-expression"?

Elitism's a dead-end road –
look at the grim stones left

by those who've tried to travel along it!
You should realise, boy,

that you owe us, that we've got you in an armlock,
that you'll compose what we want, or nothing.

Fugue on DSCH

Don't symphonies cause havoc!
Look at me, there on the platform, so
distracted, such a caricature. How else
dare I show a creature hidden? Now
I'm like a puppet, twitching and blinking
as the Party pulls at my strings.
Damaged shell, crushed and hurting,
remind me of who I am. I'm a dark
horse, a dark, secret, cryptic horse.
It's all dumb show, clues, hints.
No, don't bother looking. My posture says –
this isn't a person. I am aping Party Man.
Listen to my bones: for on this framework
Dmitri Shostakovich composes himself.

Prelude of the Apparatchiks for Babi Yar

Don't you know, there's no (oh, no no), no
taint of anti-Semitism in Russia?
We don't hate Jews. But don't dare to say
that, as much as them, we didn't suffer.
Have they got the monopoly of pain, are they
the only chosen people? Look here, we've got
our destiny too, and our problems. We don't hate
them. But we don't have too much pity to spare,
and what there is is worn as thin as the hair
on an old babushka's fanny. No welcome there!

And if there's kudos in being massacred
we want our share.

Fugue
Gravissime

Most of my symphonies are tombstones.
Even without inscriptions
I know, and they know, who they are.
They've paid the price. They're beyond further ills.
I'm walking on the dead. They can't be hurt
any more, surely. Yet in spite of myself
I stretch myself face downwards to spread the weight,
inch forwards moving my limbs with painful care.
It's like artificial respiration – too late!
Or the act of love. Yes, the love that lies
heart to heart and bone to bone.
I have laid out their bones in five rows:
and I lean on my pen until
my purple ink – their hearts'-blood – flows.

Interlude

He was like a little boy at football matches – jumped up and down, yelled, waved his arms about. His excitement was intense, but he never raised his voice nor lost that incredible reserve. It was an idealised version of the game he longed for, honourable, chivalrous, and ecstatic.

The beauty, the skill of it! And if you can't do it yourself, the next best thing is to watch, as the ball leaves the boot to go cleanly and sweetly between the posts. I admire those who can do the physical things so well. All I've ever been able to do is compose, and play the piano, and now my hand's failing.

Can you imagine, after the pleasure of spending an evening on the train chatting to such a wonderful violinist, the horror of his being discovered dead in his berth next morning? And I was the last person who saw him alive! So, they questioned me, questioned me; finally had to let me go. Then Vissarion and I went to the match together.

Remember, my friend, how I phoned you up and described the Zenith-Spartak match to you, because you couldn't be there in the flesh? That was the next best thing. And yet it was like drinking water and pretending it was export-quality vodka. So we'd always make a point of going together whenever we could.

The kids would be playing outside, having a kickabout, and he'd come out and say: *Can I have a go?* Then, after playing with them for a while, he'd suddenly disappear indoors, for maybe forty minutes or so; then back outside kicking around again ... I can think while I'm messing about with a football. It occupies the top layer of my mind with the sheer physical exercise, with the angles and trajectories, even with the purely practical problem of keeping my glasses secure on my nose, while the music moves on underneath until it gets to the point where it comes clear. Then I go inside and write it down.

Prelude

Well, we're all in the same boat. This
is the Brotherhood of Pain and Grief,

which makes you wonder what *they* mean by
'Music for Brotherhood'. The *Ode to Joy*

presumably, like that 1919 performance
when the music-lovers in the audience

were joined by sailors of the Baltic Fleet,
and the brass-players' lips froze, in spite

of the warmth of all that Brotherhood,
to their metal mouthpieces. O ye millions

I embrace you under the shadow of fear.

Fugue
Sotto voce

To compose only what you want to compose
is to test the boundaries of politics,
the half-life of fear. Listen, there is no
shield against this radiation-sickness,
lead will not help you here. Just give me
a packet of fags and some half-decent vodka
and let me get on with my work.

I haven't forgotten you, though,
people of the half-shadows. We are all
under threat, and we need a *sotto voce* anthem.
There are secret songs, melodies in the inner
voices, for those with ears to hear.
If you're not sure of the words, hum,
hum the tune with me, quietly, quietly.

Underground

I have become my own dark lantern
to light me as I mine a seam of sorrow,
for rage will burst out from a candle's gutter,
run along veins, a shock of searing flame.

I need to see where to put my feet
but cannot bear to look around too closely.
Unshielded, I might explode into grief,
torching a dangerous conflagration.

The soul always burns with the fiercest heat.

Tunguska Incident

I was two years old at the time and my life
might have been crushed out almost before I'd begun –
but all it felled was pines, felled and splintered
lying with feet towards the impact
as if to the heat of the stove on a frozen night

> *pick the spillikin trunks up one by one*
> *build me a dacha from this matchwood*

a comet fragment   a chunk of ice
becoming fireballblastwavescorchingwind
light burned the sky the earth shook –
could it have been *him* practising
ready for felling people like so many trees

> *pick their spillikin bones up one by one*
> *make me a coffin from this ivory*

deep in Siberia who knows what's going on
there are shocks that don't illuminate the sky
that aren't visible five hundred miles away –
and *he* has felled so many   oh so many
deep in the forest where the trees hide

Prelude on the Zdanov Decree

They know so much about music, these officials,
bureaucrats, Party men. And they know about power.
You mustn't ever be seen not to act;
but it has to be in waltz time – One Two Three
and all heads above the parapet together.
Pack instinct gathers its own momentum,
needs a scapegoat, an aunt sally.
So: a decree, full of long words:

> For distorting our Soviet realities
> for not reflecting our glorious victories
> for eating out of the hands of our enemies

Censured

> For unhealthy individualism
> for formalism and pessimism
> for intractable recidivism

Censured

> For despising the people with these ugly sounds
> of self-centred aestheticism
> that reject our national musical character
> under the banner of illusory innovation

You are to bear extreme censure.

Fugue

You are a vicious formalist, they said.
And, tightrope-walking over the abyss,
I am reduced to envying the dead.

They know so much. They say they know my breed,
the perpetrator of such ugly noise.
You are a vicious formalist, they said.

Yet every night my music-paper's spread
because the need to work's so strong a force
though I'm reduced to envying the dead.

There's not a tremor in the solo's thread.
But I know where it was, the very place
where they pronounced me formalist, and said

concertos and the like would not be played.
Music's Siberia! such hearts of ice!
I am reduced to envying the dead,

even the ones who died before they should
under our Soviet realities,
like me such vicious formalists (they said)
reduced to envying the dead.

Tenth Symphony

Each symphony's a world: continents, poles,
prevailing winds, its own habitual climate.

And this one is in love with her. It howls
her name through wildernesses, desolate

as desert lands. Elmira lives! it calls
a dozen times through my uneasy art –

for it's the symphony that needs her, bawls
and keens, wanting my temporary heart.

But seasons change, the waxwings will migrate
back to their breeding-grounds when instinct pulls.

Another work will need another state,
a different icon for its inner soul,

to be its heartfelt life, its personal fate.
Each muse is goddess while the artist kneels,

and Dmitri Shostakovich counterfeits
himself afresh as every work enthralls.

Recitative

A sudden death?

No.

Only to those who had failed to see
how all through that last summer
she was already
embracing her own final winter

moving
into the steps of the climb
that would take her up

over the known foothills
ascending
the mountains above Yerevan

where
she will be attenuated to birdbone

where
suddenly
she is flying

flying

the sky so clear blue a silk sheet
over her

Arioso

I never kissed her goodbye,
not properly, not for ever,
thinking she would be gone only a few weeks.

But when we reached her bedside
it was already too late.

Now she's back home, cradled in the coffin,
with me and yet not with me.
And we tiptoe round the flat
as though we were afraid to wake her final rest.

But she is deafened by the zinc lining.
I whisper to her but she doesn't hear.

Too late after that frantic flight
too late.

Lament

The sky is too grey and hard to cry
as we stand here in the colours of grief
(white snow, black clothes and red-rimmed eyes)
and it's too cold for speeches. Let's be brief.

I stand here in the colours of grief
with my motherless children. What can we do?
It's too cold for speeches. Let's be brief,
this is the place, and the place for me too,

and what will my motherless children do?
My voice is thick with frozen tears.
Here's the place, a place for me too
I whisper to her; but she doesn't hear,

my voice is thick with frozen tears.
(White snow, black clothes and red-rimmed eyes.)
I whisper to her, but she doesn't hear,
and the sky is too grey and hard to cry.

A Scapegoat

All art needs to be free.
I've sometimes thought
of suicide, come very near,

driven to wondering whether they might
ease up on the work if I wasn't there
handy for taking the role of scapegoat.

So, do I believe in a God? No,
and I am very sorry for it.
We could all do with a deity to cry to

but with so many ways of being wrong
we will have to cry silently for now
until in the words of the old saying

God forgives Russia and all the bells will ring.

Prelude after Akhmatova
Adagio molto

Three things sustained them

    the soul of the people
    the soil under their feet
    the salt of irony

and three almost undid them

    the whisper in the night
    the cries of silenced voices
    leaders with icy hearts

and Russia's winters are long

Fugue
Mesto

Not demons but despairs. I can't
speak of them, they are Siberia,
where bones dance with icicles.
But my sisters are still calling: Mitya,
never mind them! play us a foxtrot!
I'll play to them on a bone xylophone
with hammers made of ice.
There are cities on those plains
I dare not enter – they are the places
where music freezes before it's born.
And I'm a pillar of salt, the unwept tears
marking the stopping-place, saying
I refuse to go that way.

Prelude

The Little Spring
softens the air, tempts all the buds to break

the ice begins to crack
the rivers flow

and look!
things are already easier for you

but don't relax too soon –
Winter still hides a knife behind his back.

Here is the paper.
Here is the pen.

Mirror Fugue

The truly-dead are those that are forgot,
and a man without a memory's a dead man.
He will tell you everything he can.
Friends, relatives, acquaintances, the never-met –

their fates still bruise him. Listen:
the slow drips of tears, of heartbreak,
freeze and refreeze. His grief is glazed
as Leningrad's winter waterways
deepen, deepen by reflection
till the ice is far too thick to crack.

He sees their faces through his frozen tears
and finds himself mirrored with them.
You want him to sing under this ice?
today he has only the one theme.

*

Today I have only one theme.
You want me to sing under this ice
and find myself, mirrored with them?
I see their faces through my frozen tears

(this ice which is far too thick to crack)
deepened, deepened by reflection,
as Leningrad's winter waterways
freeze and refreeze. My grief is glazed
in the slow drip of tears, of heartbreak.
Their fates bruise me still. Listen,

friends, relatives, acquaintances, the never-met,
I will tell you everything I can,
for a man without a memory's a dead man.
Truly, the dead are those that are forgot.

Two-part Invention

You ghost my life
incompletely   in words

       Of course it's incomplete,
       there are translation problems –
       I can only do my best.

listen   it's the anacrusis
the upbeat   the inbreath
that's what you sing on
everything   elisions   caesurae
long phrases whole movements
all the times when melody comes hardest
everything
begins and follows through from that breath –

       I was told this years ago. I've learned it too
       from poets, who handle words
       flexible rhythms   phrasings   tied
       notes across bar lines   rests   counterpoint
       of words.

Look   you block the form out
first. In your head.

>   Gaps   cause difficulties. I relied
>   on the ear to carry the music. And lost
>   my nerve. Did you, ever?

How do I write
    for those who are oppressed?

If it were only myself
    my voice would never falter

How can I speak
    for those who died?

Fugue of the Former Students of Shostakovich against the So-Called Heroes of Their Re-Education
Allegro furioso

Tonight the phone-wires are so hot
all the birds are burning their bums –
because we've been playing Shostakovich in secret,
and now we're drunken-brave on the quartets.

Who first reached for the phone?

Call yourselves music-teachers? There's not an ear
between the lot of you!

                                          (let me have a go)

You're shit on the shoes!

                         (slam the phone down and giggle)

Arse lickers! turd eaters!

                             (two of us shouting at once)

Turd lickers! arse eaters!

                          (now we're all joining in, helpless)

Putrid spittle of a tubercular beggar!

                     (we're laughing so hard we're dribbling)

You'd fuck your own grandmothers!
even the women among you!

                                              (we're hysterical)

You're all the way up to your balls in blood!

        and suddenly it isn't funny any more.

Stalin as Heldentenor
Largo e nobilmente

What would you want with presidents and tsars?
Look! I bestride this whole great land of ours
from north to south, from utmost east to west.
I am the boss, because I know what's best
for all of you. You are my children now.
I punish and reward as fathers do,
chastise the wilful and the insolent,
teach the mistaken, spare the penitent.
Nothing of this is for myself. This blood
flows for the country's and the people's good.

The Death of Stalin

I want to be loved
was what he didn't say, our Great Leader and Teacher.
But it was what he meant all right.

No one was to be more popular –
and if he couldn't manage popular
feared would do.

Then, thinking the snapping jaws
of challengers would bite at his ankles,
shut himself up in his dacha,

had his guards outside circling
constantly, dizzily
on skis or on bicycles

guarding his power.
But the old wolf still had his teeth,
his growl still got them all cowering.

Except for Maria Yudina, she didn't care
– she had her God, and Mozart.
He sent her money; she gave it away,

said she'd pray for him in his great sin.
Loneliness
and superstition moved in him at her playing.

Send me that recording you broadcast.
And the orchestra with trembling hands
assembled, the conductor fainting was replaced

again, and again, hardly able to stand
under the threat of that vicious whimsy;
and she playing on quite unconcerned.

One recording only
of her message to him. He repeated it to himself
and died, they say,

to the clicking of the needle
in the expired groove.

The Pupil Remembers

It was his writing hand that failed him, later,
with the paralysis. It's hard not to see
that as some sort of judgement.

But did he betray the music? The incandescence
which first drew us was still undimmed through gathering clouds.
And what you must realise about real music
is, it's still there even when it seems to be lying quietly
in a drawer somewhere, when there's no performance
and no hope of any performance.
It occupies the air, it glows, it feeds,
it bursts out stronger.

If they weren't going to snuff him out altogether
they should never have tried to contain him.

There were those of us who saw him as a god.
We hung on his every word –
a teacher who'd believe in you, guide
your talents, support your work.
We'd have walked through fire for him.

                                      And then he signed
that iniquitous paper.

We'd thought he'd never give way
but all of a sudden he seemed to lose his nerve
and you saw he wasn't a young man any more.

He had been a beacon to us, which burned, saying:
Art has nothing to do with propaganda,
only with the flame of the human spirit;
a Prometheus
until he betrayed himself, betrayed us, by putting
his name to that paper.

Soliloquy

This is my country, my people, my nation.
I'd never, like some, abandon my own home soil;
but face it, we're under occupation.

And don't talk to me about internal exile.
Okay, they haven't sent me to the gulags,
bodily. Times I could welcome it, while

my soul shivers in the house of my bones;
though sometimes I can scaffold myself, compose
my own bones and the lost bones

from the dreadful pits. This is my business,
and hardly a matter for rejoicing. How long
will we be able to carry on like this,

like Jews made to dance before execution,
stumbling with exhaustion on their own graves, trying
not to put a foot wrong and go down?

Before you go to the doctor, wash the wrong
foot. Then the surgeon will amputate,
in error, the dirty, not the healthy one.

My father was forty-seven when he died.
However you look at it, I'm on borrowed time.
Angina lays siege to my heart, yet it beats

like the pedal-point of the metronome's
pacemaker, broadcast by Radio Leningrad
during the siege, in gaps between programmes,

just to show that everything was still
there, still on air, still sounding
while my purple ink froze in its well.

Don't bother about the metronome markings,
they're always wrong. You have to go by the feel:
everything's still there, still working.

Woke up this morning, couldn't hear my heart.
Woke up this morning, couldn't feel my heart
– lose the beat and the music don't start.

Myself is so difficult to believe in;
but the work – that's another matter.
As long as I can go on living

the pulse of my work won't falter.
Though I lost courage when they rubbished that,
came near to topping myself, shattered.

Once there was a sparrow that shat
on my symphony. Little innocent
creature. All it left was a crotchet.

Chaconne

Dominant to tonic   that rising fourth
opens my final fugue with a closing cadence

no accidentals   I am delaying modulation
as long as possible

let me not be transposed yet

the music breathes calmly

how to steady
the heartbeat   the pulse

        *

he was dying from the right hand
his death spreading   slowly   through him

Fedya   can you sustain
that high E   yes   like that

the holy triangle
composer   player   listener

viola's threnody
last work   last   will
I am   still   Shostakovich

        *

his face painted like a puppet
laid away in its box
slack-stringed   beyond State control

    he was still Shostakovich

official black suits bustling about
he was a true Communist
but that was not why the people wept

    he was still Shostakovich

listen
listen to his bones
right up to the final barline

    he is still Shostakovich

CODA

this is not a political statement
not the cry of a soul

it is a piece of paper
with marks on

to be realised
into another kind of surface

a temporal screen of sound
a web of textured time

and behind it is also time
make what you will of it

Biographical note

JOANNA BOULTER was born in 1942 and grew up in Wiltshire. She studied at London University, where she read Music, English and Latin, graduating in 1963. After a brief teaching career, she worked for a typesetting firm, then on marriage lived for two years in Singapore and Malaysia. A civilian posting to Teheran followed, and then she and her family returned to the UK, where she began writing again after several years' gap. After living in various parts of the country, each a little further north, she has now settled in Darlington, and finds the NE region very supportive of its writers.

Her poetry has earned her a Tyrone Guthrie Fellowship from Northern Arts, a Northern Promise award from New Writing North, and a Hawthornden Fellowship. In 2002 she gained an MA in Writing Poetry, with Distinction, from Newcastle University, and the following year won first prize in the Poetry London competition. Previous publications include three pamphlets: *Running With The Unicorns*, from The Bay Press (1994), *On Sketty Sands* (2001), and *The Hallucinogenic Effects of Breathing* (2003), both from Arrowhead Press. She is a founder member of the Darlington women's writing co-operative Vane Women, teaches a women's writing class, and works as an editor.

Twenty Four Preludes and Fugues on Dmitri Shostakovich is her first full-length collection.

Recent titles in Arc Publications'
POETRY FROM THE UK / IRELAND,
edited by Jo Shapcott, include:

LIZ ALMOND
The Shut Drawer

JONATHAN ASSER
Outside The All Stars

DONALD ATKINSON
In Waterlight: Poems New, Selected & Revised

THOMAS A CLARK
The Path to the Sea

TONY CURTIS
What Darkness Covers
The Well in the Rain

JULIA DARLING
Sudden Collapses in Public Places
Apology for Absence

KATHERINE GALLAGHER
Circus-Apprentice

CHRISSIE GITTINS
Armature

MICHAEL HASLAM
The Music Laid Her Songs in Language
A Sinner Saved by Grace

JOEL LANE
Trouble in the Heartland

HERBERT LOMAS
The Vale of Todmorden

PETE MORGAN
August Light

IAN POPLE
An Occasional Lean-to

SUBHADASSI
peeled

MICHELENE WANDOR
Musica Transalpina

JACKIE WILLS
Fever Tree